BEGINNING
SIGN LANGUAGE
SERIES

An Alphabet of
Animal Signs

by S. Harold Collins

Illustrated in part by Kathy Kifer and Dahna Solar

Special thanks to the Larson Family
for their help and knowledge.

Published by
Garlic Press
606 Powers St
Eugene, OR 97402

ISBN 0-931993-65-2
Order No. GP-065
Printed in China

www.garlicpress.com

An Alphabet of Animal Signs is organized to present an animal sign for each letter of the alphabet. Standard animal signs are largely used; but for several letters of the alphabet common animal signs are difficult to identify. Thus animals such as jay, newt, ox or yak reflect an interpretation

We hope you will enjoy the beauty and language of this book. It is yet another addition to our Beginning Sign Language Series.

Alligator

Bear

Cat
(Stroke whiskers)

Dog
(Snap fingers and pat leg)

Elephant

Frog
(Shows throat puffing)

Giraffe
(Shows long neck)

Horse
(Show ear flapping)

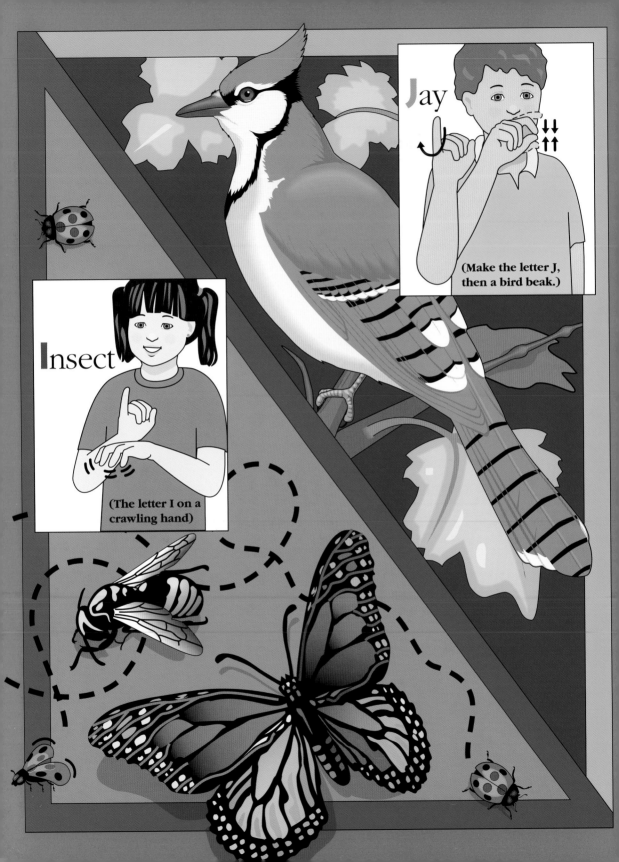

Jay

(Make the letter J,
then a bird beak.)

Insect

(The letter I on a
crawling hand)

Kangaroo

Lion

Monkey

Newt

Parrot

Owl

Rabbit

Quail

(A bird beak,
then the letter Q)

Sheep

(Use a scissors motion to "shear" your arm.)

Tiger

(Draw stripes across your cheeks)

Unicorn

Vulture

Wolf

(Stroke your long nose.)

oX
(The letters O and X)

Yak
(Use the letter
Y as a horn.)

1
2

Zebra